Beyond the Tics

Living Well with Tourette's

Rossana Lewis

TABLE OF cONTENT

Chapter 1: Understanding Tourette Syndrome

1.1 Defining Tourette Syndrome

Tourette Syndrome (TS) is a condition of the nervous system. TS causes people to have "tics". Tics are sudden twitches, movements, or sounds that people do repeatedly. People who have tics cannot stop their bodies from doing these things. For example, a person might keep blinking over and over. Or, a person might make a grunting sound unwillingly. Having tics is a little bit like having hiccups. Even though you might not want to hiccup, your body does it anyway. Sometimes people can stop themselves from doing a certain tic for a while, but it's hard. Eventually, the person has to do the tic. Depending on the type of tics a person has, and how long the tics last, a person might be diagnosed with Tourette syndrome or another type of tic disorder.

Types of Tics

There are two types of tics—motor and vocal.

Motor Tics: Motor tics are movements of the body. Examples of motor tics include blinking, shrugging the shoulders, or jerking an arm.

Vocal Tics: Vocal tics are sounds that a person makes with his or her voice. Examples of vocal tics include humming, clearing the throat, or yelling out a word or phrase.

Tics can be either simple or complex:

Simple Tics: Simple tics involve just a few parts of the body. Examples of simple tics include squinting the eyes or sniffing.

Complex Tics: Complex tics usually involve several different parts of the body and can have a pattern. An example of a complex tic is bobbing the head while jerking an arm, and then jumping up.

1.2 Myths and Misconceptions

There are many common misconceptions about Tourette syndrome as it pertains to its origin, symptoms and treatment. Due to a lack of understanding, there are numerous myths surrounding Tourette's. It is important to address and correct Tourette syndrome misconceptions to decrease confusion and prejudice.

Myth 1: Everyone with Tourette's blurts out obscenities.

FACT: Only a small percentage of people with Tourette syndrome blurt out obscenities.

Coprolalia is the extreme and uncontrolled use of curses, obscenities and offensive remarks. Despite common misperceptions, only 32 percent of people with Tourette syndrome experience coprolalia. Coprolalia is an intense vocal tic that can entail inappropriate or socially unacceptable comments or expressions in public. Individuals are unable to control their cursing, as it is involuntary, unintentional and not under their conscious control. People are often embarrassed and upset when outbursts occur and commonly try to cover them up. Tourette syndrome and swearing are commonly linked together, which is likely due to the fact that it is one of the most highlighted symptoms on television and movies. This portrayal has contributed to the incorrect stereotype.

Myth 2: Everyone who has tics also has Tourette syndrome.

FACT: Just because a person has tics does not mean that they also have Tourette syndrome.

You can have tics without having Tourette syndrome. Tic conditions occur widely on a spectrum, ranging from minor and temporary to more complex and permanent. Temporary tics can last for several weeks or months and may then resolve themselves, while more severe tics can be enduring, disabling and impact several areas of the body. Tourette syndrome is the most severe form of tic disorders. Less severe forms include persistent motor tic disorder, persistent vocal tic disorder and provisional tic disorder. Other syndromes and diseases that may cause tics include Huntington disease and cerebral palsy. Tics may result from head trauma injuries or certain types of medications.

Myth 3: People with Tourette's can control their tics if they really want to.
FACT: Tics are involuntary and uncontrollable for someone with Tourette syndrome.

Controlling Tourette syndrome is impossible, as people cannot control urges on their own. Tics stem from a neurological issue involving altered brain functioning and changed brain structure, which makes tics completely involuntary. Some individuals with Tourette syndrome are able to control tics and twitches for brief periods, but this requires a significant amount of focus and concentration. The delaying and inhibiting of tics are temporary and fleeting. The only reliable way to control tics is through behavior therapies and medications.

Myth 4: Tourette's is caused by an unhappy childhood.

FACT: Tourette syndrome is not brought on by an unhappy childhood.

Tourette syndrome causes are currently unknown, although it is believed that there is a hereditary and genetic component. Environmental factors, autoimmune issues and the prenatal environment are also hypothesized to contribute to the progression of the syndrome. While stress has the potential to worsen symptoms, it is never the originating cause. Despite the fact that what causes Tourette syndrome is still unspecified, an unhappy childhood is not one of the potential possibilities.

Myth 5: Tics only occur in children
FACT: Tics can occur in children, adolescents, adults and the elderly.

Tics can be present in all age groups and are not only linked to childhood. Tourette syndrome is a neurodevelopmental disorder that impacts the nervous system. Most symptoms first occur in childhood around the age of 7 and peak between the ages of 10 and 12. The worst symptoms usually occur before the age of 18. Symptoms present in childhood do have the potential to reduce or lessen in intensity with age, but many symptoms can remain the same and continue into adulthood. The vast majority of children with Tourette syndrome go on to develop into adults with the condition.

Approximately 1 in 100 people have tic disorders, including adults. Although rare, tics can start in adulthood and later in life. There are many types of tics in adults that are permanent and severe. Tourette syndrome in adults can range widely from milder to more serious. By adolescence and young adulthood, many indivduals have no tics, less than 50% have mild tics and less than 25% have moderate to severe tics. Most medical practitioners that specialize in Tourette's work with children and do not continue providing treatment to patients as they become older. This can result in an untreated and unaccounted part of the adult population, which may contribute to the misconception that tics can only occur in children.

Myth 6: People with Tourette's can't be athletes.

FACT: People with Tourette syndrome can become athletes and have successful careers.

Individuals with Tourette syndrome can develop skills, play sports and become athletes. Some individuals have even found that their tics lessen when they put intense focus into a task. People with Tourette's can enjoy sports, whether they choose to play competitively or recreationally. Many athletes with Tourette syndrome have done extremely well in sports and have gone on to have successful professional careers. For example, Jim Eisenreich was a successful Major League baseball player who went to the World Series, Mahmoud Abdul-Rauf played basketball for the NBA and and Tim Howard was a soccer star that played in the World Cup tournament.

All of these individuals had Tourette's and were still able to perform as athletes successfully.

Myth 7: Tourette's is extremely rare.
FACT: Tourette's has a relatively high prevalence.

When considering how common Tourette syndrome is, it is important to note that it is much more prevalent than people believe it to be. The prevalence of Tourette syndrome was once believed to be relatively rare, but this is no longer accurate. It is estimated that about 1 in 160 children between the ages of 5 and 17 in the United States are diagnosed with Tourette's, with a total of 300,000 children impacted.

It is believed that at least 50% of children with Tourette syndrome go undiagnosed, suggesting that the prevalence of Tourette syndrome is underreported. Tourette syndrome statistics show that the syndrome impacts about 6 in 1,000 individuals, including adults.

Myth 8: All Tourette syndrome patients have anger management issues.
FACT: Individuals with Tourette's may have angry outbursts, but do not always have anger management issues.

Another common misconception pertains to Tourette syndrome and anger. Individuals with Tourette's can experience a phenomenon called "Rage Attacks," which are characterized by sudden explosions of rage and anger. These abrupt and sudden outbursts occur in about 25% of children. These attacks are not attention seeking or goal-directed and instead are believed to be involuntary. The common association between Tourette syndrome and anger outbursts are another result of inaccurate media portrayal in television and movies.

Myth 9: If I can't see the tics, they must be doing better.
FACT: When tics are lessened, it does not mean that Tourette syndrome is gone or that the condition has been resolved.

Individuals with Tourette syndrome can attempt to repress or hold back their tics, but this does not mean that their condition has resolved. The lessening of tics does not mean that a person is doing better or that they are instantaneously healed and treated.

Myth 10: People with Tourette syndrome can't live normal lives.

FACT: Individuals with Tourette syndrome can lead full and fulfilling lives.

Living with Tourette syndrome can be challenging, but it does not have to stop a person from living a happy, full life. Individuals can achieve success in school, friendships, relationships and careers despite having Tourette syndrome. Several celebrities including Dan Aykroyd and Michael Wolff have achieved success despite their Tourette syndrome diagnosis. Tic disorders are treatable and are responsive to treatment. Medication and therapies can help people decrease their tics to the point where they are hardly noticeable.

1.3 Causes and Diagnosis

Causes

The exact cause of Tourette syndrome remains a mystery, but research is focusing on a number of possibilities, including:

Genetic Factors: Tourette syndrome seems to be an inherited condition. A child of a person with Tourette syndrome has a 50 percent chance of developing the condition themselves. Boys are three times more likely to inherit the condition than girls.

Streptococcal Infection: the streptococcus bacteria can cause a wide range of infections, ranging from mild to severe and life threatening. One theory proposes that a particular infection may be responsible for the neurological changes associated with Tourette syndrome.

Neurochemical Abnormalities: the chemicals of the brain (neurotransmitters) seem to be metabolized differently in people with Tourette syndrome, especially the mood regulators dopamine and serotonin.

Other Disorders: researchers are divided on whether or not Tourette syndrome is associated with other disorders (such as ADHD and dyslexia) and obsessive compulsive behaviors. Such disorders often appear together with Tourette syndrome.

Diagnosis

Diagnosing Tourette syndrome primarily involves observation of the person's behavior. Since tics and vocalizations are often vented in the privacy and safety of the home, the doctor may have some initial difficulty witnessing the symptoms in a professional setting like their office or clinic.

Other tests, such as CT scans, are used to make sure the symptoms aren't caused by some other underlying disease.

Chapter 2: Exploring Tourette's Symptoms

2.1 Motor Tics: Understanding and Coping

Tourette Syndrome is often recognized by the presence of motor tics, involuntary movements that can range from subtle twitches to more noticeable gestures or actions. Understanding motor tics and implementing coping strategies can significantly help individuals manage these symptoms.

Understanding Motor Tics

Motor tics in Tourette's manifest as sudden, repetitive, and involuntary movements. They can affect various muscle groups, resulting in actions such as eye blinking, head jerking, shoulder shrugging, facial grimacing, or limb movements.

The severity and frequency of motor tics can fluctuate over time, and they may worsen in response to stress, anxiety, or excitement.

Coping Strategies

Awareness and Acceptance: Acknowledging the presence of motor tics and understanding that they are involuntary can help individuals cope better. Accepting these movements as part of Tourette's and reducing anxiety around them can be empowering.

Stress Management: Stress often exacerbates tics. Engaging in relaxation techniques like deep breathing, meditation, or yoga can help reduce stress levels, subsequently minimizing the intensity of motor tics.

Identifying Triggers: Observing and identifying triggers that worsen tics (such as certain environments, emotions, or fatigue) can assist in managing and minimizing their occurrence.

Diverting Attention: Redirecting focus onto engaging activities or hobbies can divert attention away from tics, potentially reducing their frequency. Engaging in activities that require concentration or physical movement might offer temporary relief.

Environmental Modifications: Making adjustments in the environment, such as reducing clutter or creating a comfortable space, can alleviate stress and potentially decrease tic frequency.

Seeking Support: Seeking support from friends, family, or support groups can provide comfort and understanding, fostering an environment where individuals with Tourette's feel accepted and supported.

2.2 Vocal Tics: Managing challenges

Vocal tics, a defining characteristic of Tourette Syndrome, encompass involuntary sounds or utterances, varying from simple noises to complex words or phrases.

Managing Challenges

Awareness and Acceptance: Acknowledging that vocal tics are involuntary and beyond personal control can aid in self-acceptance. Accepting these tics as part of Tourette's and reducing self-consciousness about them can be empowering.

Relaxation Techniques: Practicing relaxation methods, such as deep breathing exercises, meditation, or progressive muscle relaxation, can reduce stress and anxiety levels, potentially lessening the occurrence or intensity of vocal tics.

Environmental Adaptations: Creating supportive surroundings by informing close contacts about Tourette's can alleviate stress associated with vocal tics. Promoting understanding and empathy can contribute to a more comfortable environment.

Speech and Behavioral Therapies: Working with a speech therapist or behavioral specialist experienced in Tourette's can provide valuable techniques to manage vocal tics. Therapy sessions might involve breathing exercises, vocal control methods, or habit reversal techniques.

Community Support: Engaging with support groups or connecting with others facing similar challenges can provide valuable emotional support. Sharing experiences and strategies can foster a sense of solidarity and understanding.

2.3 Other Associated Symptoms

Tourette Syndrome is characterized not only by motor and vocal tics but can also present with a range of associated symptoms that individuals may experience in varying degrees.

Obsessive-Compulsive Symptoms (OCD) and Attention-Deficit/Hyperactivity Disorder (ADHD): Many individuals with Tourette's often experience co-occurring conditions such as OCD or ADHD. OCD may involve persistent thoughts or behaviors, like repetitive actions or intrusive thoughts. ADHD symptoms can encompass difficulties with focus, hyperactivity, and impulsivity. Managing these associated conditions often requires a tailored approach that might include therapy, medication, or a combination of both.

Anxiety and Emotional Challenges: Anxiety disorders, including social anxiety or generalized anxiety, are prevalent among individuals with Tourette Syndrome. Coping with the challenges of tics, potential social stigmatization, or disruptions in daily life due to symptoms can contribute to heightened anxiety levels. Learning effective coping mechanisms and seeking support are essential in managing anxiety and emotional challenges.

Sensory Sensitivities: Some individuals with Tourette's may experience sensory sensitivities, such as heightened sensitivity to sounds, textures, or certain visual stimuli. Understanding and managing these sensitivities by minimizing exposure or employing sensory strategies can help alleviate discomfort.

Sleep Disorders: Sleep disturbances, including difficulties falling asleep, maintaining sleep, or experiencing restless sleep, are commonly reported by individuals with Tourette Syndrome. These disruptions might result from tics interfering with sleep or coexisting conditions. Implementing good sleep hygiene practices can assist in improving sleep quality.

Mood Disorders: Depression or mood fluctuations are observed in some individuals with Tourette's. Coping with the challenges posed by Tourette Syndrome, especially when accompanied by social stigma, can impact mental health. Seeking professional support for managing mood-related symptoms is crucial.

Chapter 3: Navigating Life with Tourette's

3.1 Living with Tourette's

Patients living with Tourette syndrome can have difficulty integrating into society and coping with daily activities, as a result of the syndrome. Fortunately, the majority of patients will find that their symptoms subside within approximately ten years. One in three patients tends to suffer from the condition for their lifetime, although the severity typically reduces as they get older, reducing their reliance on medications and other management techniques.

A number of techniques can help in the management of the condition and improve the quality of life for the individual substantially.

Most individuals with Tourette syndrome find that they are able to suppress their tics for a certain amount of time. However, restraining the tics for a long period of time is not thought to be beneficial as it is difficult and tiring for the individual. For this reason, it is best if they are able to release the tic as soon as possible to reduce the severity of the episode.

In many cases, patients are able to reduce the frequency and severity of tics significantly with the use of self-help tips and simple lifestyle changes.

These include:

- Avoidance of stressful situations that may trigger a tic
- Availability of a "calm room" to release the tic away from other individuals.

- Involvement in a supportive community (in person or online) to connect with individuals with similar issues.

- Partaking in high-concentration activities, such as playing an instrument or competitive sport.

3.2 School and Work: Thriving in Educational and Professional Settings

Navigating school or the workplace with Tourette Syndrome can feel like a unique journey. These environments come with their challenges, but with the right strategies and a supportive community, excelling is absolutely possible.

Making School More Accommodating

First off, it's crucial to create an understanding space at school. This involves informing teachers and classmates about Tourette's to clear up any misunderstandings. Sharing insights on the condition can foster empathy and reduce stigma. Plus, it opens the door for some helpful accommodations, like seating preferences or taking short breaks during class.

School also offers Individualized Education Plans (IEPs) or 504 Plans, tailored to suit specific needs. These plans can provide extra time during tests, a quieter setting for exams, or the chance to record lessons for better focus. Encouraging peer support is a gem too! Initiatives led by students or support groups among classmates can create an inclusive atmosphere, which is invaluable for anyone dealing with Tourette's.

Thriving in the Working World

Transitioning to the professional realm can present similar challenges. Deciding whether to disclose Tourette's at work is a personal call. But educating bosses and colleagues about the condition can be a game-changer. It can break down barriers and create an environment where understanding and collaboration thrive.

Asking for accommodations that suit individual needs—like a quieter workspace or flexible schedules—can significantly ease the work experience. Managing stress at work is also key. Finding strategies to handle stressors and organizing tasks better can help manage tics effectively.

And it's not just about the work! Engaging in professional growth opportunities and networking can broaden skill sets and build supportive professional relationships.

3.3 Social Relationships and Tourette's

Navigating social circles while dealing with Tourette Syndrome can be a real journey. It's all about building understanding, connecting with others, and finding support within your tribe.

Opening Up the Conversation

One of the most powerful tools is open communication. Talking about Tourette's with friends, family, or new folks you meet can lighten the mood. Sharing your experiences, even tossing in a bit of humor about those tics, can create a relaxed atmosphere where everyone feels at ease.

It's All About Empathy

Empathy is pure magic in any relationship. Encouraging the people in your life to learn more about Tourette's goes a long way. When friends or family show empathy and acceptance during those tic moments, it's like a warm blanket on a cold day.

Finding Your Comfort Zone

Social situations can sometimes feel like a whirlwind. But discovering what helps ease stress—whether it's finding a cozy spot or having a buddy who understands your need for space during intense tic moments—can make socializing more enjoyable.

Quality Over Quantity

In the world of friendships, it's not about the numbers game. It's about those special connections. Having a circle of understanding friends or a supportive network is way more meaningful than having a crowd around you. The real deal lies in those connections that celebrate your uniqueness.

Strength in Numbers

Joining support groups or communities with folks going through similar experiences can be a game-changer. It's a space where sharing stories, swapping tips, and lifting each other up happens, creating this amazing sense of togetherness.

Chapter 4: Treatment Approaches and Therapies

4.1 Medications and Their Role

Medications to help control tics or reduce symptoms of related conditions include:

Medications that Block or Lessen Dopamine: Fluphenazine, haloperidol (Haldol), risperidone (Risperdal) and pimozide (Orap) can help control tics. Possible side effects include weight gain and involuntary repetitive movements. Tetrabenazine (Xenazine) might be recommended, although it may cause severe depression.

Botulinum (Botox) Injections: An injection into the affected muscle might help relieve a simple or vocal tic.

ADHD Medications: Stimulants such as methylphenidate (Metadate CD, Ritalin LA, others) and medications containing dextroamphetamine (Adderall XR, Dexedrine, others) can help increase attention and concentration. However, for some people with Tourette syndrome, medications for ADHD can exacerbate tics.

Central Adrenergic Inhibitors: Medications such as clonidine (Catapres, Kapvay) and guanfacine (Intuniv) — typically prescribed for high blood pressure — might help control behavioral symptoms such as impulse control problems and rage attacks. Side effects may include sleepiness.

Antidepressants: Fluoxetine (Prozac, Sarafem, others) might help control symptoms of sadness, anxiety and OCD.

Antiseizure Medications: Recent studies suggest that some people with Tourette syndrome respond to topiramate (Topamax), which is used to treat epilepsy.

4.2 Behavioral Therapies: CBIT (Comprehensive Behavioral Information for Tics)

CBIT is a type of behavioral therapy that teaches a person to become aware of their behavior and helps them change how they behave. It is very systematic and carefully planned, depending on each person's specific needs and symptoms, and typically takes place in a therapist's office.

During CBIT, the therapist helps individuals with tics learn to

- Become more aware of their tics and the urge to tic
- Carefully choose and practice a new behavior instead of the tic. This "new behavior" (competing response) helps reduce and, in some cases, even eliminate the tic
- Identify situations that can make tics worse and find ways to change them; and
- Learn ways to prevent or cope with stress

4.3 Alternative and Complementary Therapies

In addition to conventional treatments, some individuals explore alternative and complementary therapies to manage Tourette Syndrome symptoms. While these therapies may not be universally endorsed or scientifically proven, some find them beneficial in their journey toward symptom management and overall well-being.

Acupuncture and Acupressure: Acupuncture, a traditional Chinese medicine technique involving the insertion of thin needles into specific points on the body, and acupressure, which applies pressure to these points, have been explored by some individuals with Tourette's. Though research on their efficacy for tics remains limited, some report improvements in reducing stress and promoting relaxation.

Herbal Remedies and Supplements: Certain herbal remedies and supplements are thought to offer symptom relief. Supplements like magnesium and omega-3 fatty acids are believed to potentially alleviate tics and manage associated conditions like anxiety or ADHD. However, it's crucial to consult healthcare professionals before incorporating these into a treatment plan due to potential interactions and varying efficacy.

Mind-Body Practices: Yoga and Meditation: Mind-body practices such as yoga and meditation are often embraced for their stress-relieving benefits. These practices focus on relaxation techniques, deep breathing, and mindfulness, aiming to reduce stress levels that may exacerbate tics. While they might not directly impact tics, they can contribute to overall well-being.

Dietary Modifications: Exploring dietary changes, such as eliminating certain foods like artificial additives or gluten, is another avenue individuals explore. While scientific evidence supporting specific diets' efficacy in managing tics is inconclusive, some individuals report improvements in symptom management by identifying and eliminating potential trigger foods.

Biofeedback and Hypnotherapy: Biofeedback techniques teach individuals to control physiological processes, potentially aiding in tic management. Hypnotherapy, which involves guided relaxation and suggestion techniques, is also explored by some individuals seeking symptom relief.

It's crucial to approach alternative therapies with caution. While some find these therapies beneficial, they may not work for everyone, and their efficacy varies. Consulting healthcare professionals before integrating alternative or complementary therapies into a treatment plan is strongly advised to ensure safety and compatibility with existing treatments.

Chapter 5: Empowering Self-Management

5.1 Stress Management Techniques

Stress management is essential for people with Tourette Syndrome since it frequently makes tics worse. The degree of symptoms and general well-being can be considerably reduced by implementing efficient stress management strategies.

Mindfulness Meditation: Mindfulness meditation involves focusing attention on the present moment, fostering a state of relaxation. Practicing mindfulness regularly can help reduce stress levels, subsequently minimizing the intensity and frequency of tics. Techniques like mindful breathing or body scan meditations can be particularly helpful.

Progressive Muscle Relaxation: Progressive muscle relaxation involves tensing and relaxing different muscle groups systematically. By learning to recognize and release muscle tension, individuals can alleviate physical stress, promoting overall relaxation and potentially reducing tic occurrences.

Deep Breathing Exercises: Deep breathing exercises, such as diaphragmatic breathing or belly breathing, help activate the body's relaxation response. Engaging in these exercises during stressful moments can calm the nervous system, decrease anxiety, and potentially ease tic symptoms.

Regular Exercise and Physical Activity: Engaging in regular physical activity can effectively reduce stress levels. Exercise promotes the release of endorphins, the body's natural stress fighters, helping individuals manage stress and potentially decrease tic severity.

Healthy Lifestyle Habits: Maintaining a balanced lifestyle through proper sleep, nutritious diet, and adequate hydration is essential for stress management. Establishing a routine and ensuring sufficient rest can minimize stress, positively impacting tic frequency and intensity.

Social Support and Connection: Connecting with supportive friends, family, or support groups can alleviate stress. Having a supportive network to share experiences, seek advice, or simply offer companionship can significantly impact stress levels and overall well-being.

Time Management and Prioritization: Learning effective time management skills and setting realistic goals can reduce stress related to daily tasks. Breaking tasks into manageable chunks and prioritizing them can prevent feelings of overwhelm and stress.

5.2 Building Self-Esteem and Confidence

People with Tourette's syndrome often struggle with self-esteem and confidence issues. This is because they may feel embarrassed or ashamed of their tics, and may worry about how others will perceive them. However, there are ways for people with Tourette's to build self-esteem and confidence. Some tips include:

- Learning to accept and embrace their tics as part of who they are. People with Tourette's may feel ashamed of their tics and try to hide them, but this can be exhausting and make their tics worse. It's important to accept that tics are a normal part of the disorder and not something to be ashamed of. Once they can accept their tics, they can begin to focus on their strengths and what makes them unique.

- Focusing on their strengths and positive qualities. Everyone has strengths and unique gifts to offer the world, even people with Tourette's. They may be good at sports, art, music, academics, or something else. Focusing on their strengths can help boost their confidence and self-esteem. They can also look for ways to use their strengths to help others, which can be very rewarding.

- Surrounding themselves with supportive people who accept them for who they are. Family, friends, and teachers who understand and accept the person with Tourette's can make a big difference in how they feel about themselves. They can also look for a therapist or counselor who specializes in helping people with Tourette's. Having a supportive network of people can really boost their confidence and self-esteem.

- Practicing self-care such as relaxation techniques, exercise and healthy eating. These things may not seem directly related to self-esteem, but they can make a big difference. When a person is relaxed, they feel better about themselves. Exercise releases endorphins, which can boost mood and confidence. Eating healthy foods helps the body and mind feel good. When a person feels good physically, it can have a positive impact on their mental health.

5.3 Strategies for Daily Life Challenges

Living with Tourette Syndrome brings unique challenges, but there are strategies to help navigate daily life with greater ease and confidence.

Education and Awareness: Understanding Tourette's and educating those around you can help create a supportive environment. Sharing information about the condition with family, friends, and colleagues can foster understanding and reduce misconceptions.

Developing Coping Mechanisms: Learning effective coping mechanisms to manage tics and related challenges is empowering. Techniques like deep breathing exercises, mindfulness, or redirecting tics to less noticeable movements can help minimize the impact of tics on daily activities.

Time Management and Organization: Adopting good time management skills and organizational strategies can reduce stress. Breaking tasks into smaller, manageable steps and creating structured routines can enhance productivity and decrease anxiety.

Advocating for Accommodations: In academic or workplace settings, advocating for reasonable accommodations can be beneficial. Working with educators or employers to implement accommodations that support your needs can significantly improve daily functioning.

Social Skills and Communication: Developing strong social skills and effective communication can ease interactions with others. Practicing assertiveness and explaining Tourette's in a straightforward yet confident manner can help manage social situations.

Self-Care and Stress Management: Prioritizing self-care activities, including exercise, relaxation techniques, and hobbies, can reduce stress levels. Engaging in activities that bring joy and relaxation contributes to overall well-being.

Flexibility and Adaptability: Being flexible and adaptable to changes is crucial. Recognizing that some days may be more challenging than others and being kind to oneself during difficult times is important for mental health.

Seeking Support: Don't hesitate to seek support from therapists, support groups, or online communities. Connecting with others who understand your experiences can provide validation, advice, and emotional support.

Celebrating Achievements: Acknowledging and celebrating personal achievements, no matter how small, can boost self-esteem and provide motivation to overcome challenges.

Professional Guidance: Consulting with healthcare professionals, such as therapists or counselors specialized in Tourette Syndrome, can offer tailored strategies and guidance for managing daily challenges effectively..

Chapter 6: Nutrition and Tourette Syndrome

6.1 Dietary Considerations and Potential Triggers

Food Sensitivities and Triggers

- Common Culprits: Some individuals may notice that certain foods or additives trigger their tics or worsen their symptoms. While this varies from person to person, common triggers reported include caffeine, artificial sweeteners, food colorings, and preservatives.

- Keep a Food Diary: Encourage individuals to keep a detailed diary of their diet and tic severity to identify potential correlations between certain foods and symptom exacerbation.

Nutritional Deficiencies

- Magnesium and Vitamin B6: Some studies suggest that deficiencies in certain nutrients, like magnesium and vitamin B6, might contribute to tic severity. Ensuring an adequate intake of these nutrients through diet or supplements could be beneficial.

- Omega-3 Fatty Acids: Research indicates that omega-3 fatty acids found in fish oil may have a positive impact on reducing tic severity in some individuals.

Potential Dietary Strategies

- Balanced Diet: Encourage a balanced and nutritious diet rich in fruits, vegetables, whole grains, lean proteins, and healthy fats.

- Hydration: Staying adequately hydrated is essential. Water intake helps maintain overall health and may positively impact tic symptoms.

- Avoiding Potential Triggers: While not universal, some individuals find relief by eliminating or reducing certain foods known to exacerbate symptoms. This might include processed foods, high-sugar items, or foods with artificial additives.

- Considerations for Caffeine and Sugar: Some people report that reducing or eliminating caffeine and sugar intake helps manage their tics. This includes cutting back on coffee, energy drinks, and sugary snacks.

It's crucial to note that dietary triggers can vary significantly among individuals. What affects one person may not affect another. Encourage personalized experimentation to identify specific triggers.

6.2 Meal Plans and Recipes for Tourette Syndrome

Emphasis on Balanced Nutrition:

- Include Various Food Groups: Incorporate fruits, vegetables, whole grains, lean proteins (such as poultry, fish, tofu), and healthy fats (avocado, nuts, seeds) into meals.
- Regular Meal Times: Establish a routine with regular meal schedules to help stabilize blood sugar levels.

Potential Trigger Foods to Avoid:

- Identify and Avoid Triggers: Based on individual observations, exclude potential triggers like caffeine, artificial sweeteners, food colorings, and preservatives known to worsen symptoms.

Sample Meal Ideas:

Breakfast

- Overnight oats with mixed berries and nuts
- Veggie omelet with whole-grain toast
- Greek yogurt with honey and sliced fruits

Lunch

- Quinoa salad with grilled chicken and vegetables
- Whole-grain wrap with hummus, turkey, and veggies
- Lentil soup with a side of whole-grain bread

Dinner

- Baked salmon with roasted vegetables and quinoa
- Stir-fried tofu with brown rice and mixed vegetables
- Grilled chicken with sweet potato and steamed broccoli

Recipe Considerations

- Simple and Wholesome Recipes: Opt for recipes that use fresh, unprocessed ingredients.
- Experiment with Substitutions: Replace potential trigger ingredients with suitable alternatives (e.g., natural sweeteners instead of artificial ones).

Hydration: Ensure adequate water intake throughout the day to stay hydrated and maintain overall health.

Chapter 7: Thriving Beyond Tourette's

7.1 Success Stories and Inspirational Journeys

Linda's Success Story

This is the personal story of Linda and her son Lucas.

"We first noticed that Lucas had tics in third grade. We had our suspicion that he may have TS [Tourette Syndrome] but we were frustrated with finding a doctor who knew about TS. The tics got worse; then we finally got a diagnosis when he was in the fourth grade." As is sometimes the case, Lucas was also diagnosed with ADHD [Attention-deficit/hyperactivity disorder] and obsessive-compulsive disorder.

"He went from being a straight A student to not passing classes in middle and high school. Treatments were trial and error. Over 4 years we tried medication, which was a negative experience, and nutrition and diets, with no change. We also tried neuro-feedback which was helpful for a short time, but with no lasting improvement. Fortunately we had a friend in the TS community that recommended we go to a TSA family education program. In January, we attended the program and learned about a new way to treat TS –it was CBIT." CBIT is a type of behavioral therapy that was developed for people with tics. Behavioral therapy teaches a person to become aware of their behavior and helps them change what they do in a very careful and systematic way.

"It was a huge blessing and we saw immediate improvement. Two days after Lucas started CBIT the first tic was gone. Each week another tic was gone. Now, at 15, he is basically tic-free for the first time since third grade. If we had known about CBIT 4 years ago, it would have made the past 4 years so much better. One thing I really like about CBIT is that Lucas is learning how to handle tics, so if new ones come up, he'll be able to manage them on his own."

"I wish pediatricians and teachers knew more about TS. It is so important to identify it early on and send families in the right direction. There is a good treatment, CBIT, and it worked for us."

Mike's Success Story
"My name is Mike Higgins and I am a father, a pastor, a husband, a dean of students of a

seminary, a minister, a full colonel in the United States Army, and I have Tourette syndrome.

"The first time I heard the word, 'Tourette syndrome,' from the doctor I had no idea what he was talking about. I had never heard of it. I didn't know anybody who had ever heard of it before. There were a lot of days as a 12 year-old when I would lay in bed and think about what was happening to me that I could not control. It caused me to wonder, 'Why was I born like this?'

"I think that I was not diagnosed until I was 28 years old because our family doctors didn't know about Tourette syndrome. I had been training for three weeks in Death Valley, California, and I was really hot, really dirty, really tired, and my tics were all over the place.

My battalion commander noticed and ordered me to get checked out. Finally, I met a neurologist who asked me if anybody in my family had ever had this. I told him that my grandfather did. And he said, 'I think I know what you have.'

"I didn't think that I was ever going to be married because it seemed like it was hard enough to just be single with Tourette syndrome. But in my family life now, it's just who I am. I think that my wife Renee is such a spiritually mature woman and I still look up to her because she's been my champion in all of this, helping me along, and has really been there by my side. She has never treated me as a victim and refuses to let me be a victim.

"The churches that I've been in have very celebratory worship styles. When I'm preaching, I don't tic a lot; sometimes not at all. It seems like there's a grace period I get when I'm focused on something that I'm passionate about. If we can educate the ministers, pastors, and religious leaders about Tourette's, then they can go on to educate folks in their congregations, families of children with Tourette's, and also folks who don't understand Tourette's.

"I don't think Tourette's takes away your dreams. I just think that it may put an extra wall or two between you and accomplishing your dreams. But you can get over the walls. As I say, 'You may have Tourette syndrome, but it doesn't have to have you.'"

7.2 Pursuing Passion and Achieving Goals

Living with Tourette Syndrome doesn't limit one's ability to pursue passions and achieve dreams. Here's how individuals can navigate towards their goals while managing Tourette's challenges:

Identifying Passions: Discovering and nurturing passions is essential. Whether it's art, music, sports, or academic pursuits, identifying what brings joy and fulfillment can serve as a powerful motivator.

Setting Realistic Goals: Setting achievable and specific goals is key. Breaking down large goals into smaller, manageable steps helps create a clear path towards success, contributing to a sense of accomplishment.

Adaptation and Flexibility: Being adaptable to accommodate Tourette's challenges is crucial. Embracing flexibility and adjusting strategies when needed allows for continued progress towards goals.

Seeking Support and Mentorship: Seeking guidance from mentors or support groups can provide invaluable advice and encouragement. Connecting with individuals who have overcome similar challenges can offer inspiration and practical advice.

Utilizing Strengths: Leveraging personal strengths is empowering. Focusing on areas of strength and using them to one's advantage in pursuit of goals can boost confidence and motivation.

Developing Resilience: Cultivating resilience in the face of setbacks is vital. Understanding that setbacks are a part of any journey and using them as learning opportunities fosters resilience and determination.

Embracing Passion Projects: Engaging in passion projects or hobbies can provide a sense of purpose and joy. Devoting time to creative outlets or interests allows for a sense of accomplishment outside of set goals.

Advocacy and Inspiration: Advocating for oneself and sharing experiences can inspire others facing similar challenges. Becoming an advocate not only raises awareness but also contributes to personal growth and fulfillment.

Professional Guidance and Support Systems: Seeking advice and professional guidance, whether from therapists, career counselors, or educators, can provide strategies for managing challenges while pursuing goals.

Celebrating Milestones: Celebrating achievements, no matter how small, is important. Recognizing progress and milestones along the way provides motivation and reinforces determination.

7.3 Overcoming Stigma and Embracing Individuality

Living with Tourette Syndrome may come with challenges, including societal misconceptions and stigma. Overcoming these challenges involves embracing individuality and advocating for understanding.

Understanding Stigma: Stigma arises from misconceptions and lack of awareness. Understanding that stigma is often rooted in ignorance rather than malice can help individuals approach it with a sense of education and empowerment.

Education and Awareness: Education is a powerful tool against stigma. Sharing accurate information about Tourette Syndrome with friends, family, colleagues, and the wider community can dispel myths and foster a more inclusive and understanding environment.

Open Communication: Openly communicating about Tourette's with others is key. Sharing personal experiences, challenges, and triumphs can humanize the condition and encourage empathy, breaking down the barriers of stigma.

Building a Support Network: Creating a support network of understanding friends, family, and colleagues provides a safe space. Having individuals who champion and stand by you can be a powerful antidote to external stigma.

Advocacy for Understanding: Advocacy efforts, whether on a personal or community level, contribute to broader understanding. Engaging in conversations, participating in awareness campaigns, or even sharing personal stories online can challenge stereotypes and combat stigma.

Developing Self-Advocacy Skills: Learning to advocate for oneself is empowering. Developing the skills to confidently and assertively communicate about Tourette's allows individuals to take control of their narrative and challenge stigmatizing attitudes.

Counseling and Mental Health Support: Experiencing stigma can take a toll on mental health. Seeking counseling or mental health support provides a space to process emotions, develop coping strategies, and build resilience against the impact of societal judgments.

Embracing Individuality: Embracing individuality means accepting oneself fully, Tourette's and all. Recognizing that Tourette Syndrome is just one aspect of a multifaceted identity allows individuals to see the richness and uniqueness they bring to the world.

Promoting Inclusivity: Actively participating in activities that promote inclusivity and diversity helps reshape societal norms. Being involved in inclusive events, workplaces, and communities contributes to a more accepting and understanding society.

Cultivating Confidence: Cultivating confidence in one's abilities and strengths is a powerful way to counteract stigma. Focusing on personal achievements and talents builds resilience against external judgments.

Changing Perspectives Through Success Stories: Sharing success stories of individuals with Tourette Syndrome who have excelled in various fields can challenge stereotypes. Highlighting these achievements helps shift societal perspectives and fosters a more inclusive mindset.

If you're reading this book, Beyond the Tics, you may also be interested in my books on Alzheimer's and breast cancer. Tap the links to read them.

Thank you for purchasing my book. I'd really appreciate it if you could take a moment to leave a review. Your feedback will help me improve and make my next book even better. I'm always looking forward to improving, so please do not hold back! Thank you for your time and support.